Everyday Graces

Illustrated by Gillian Gaze

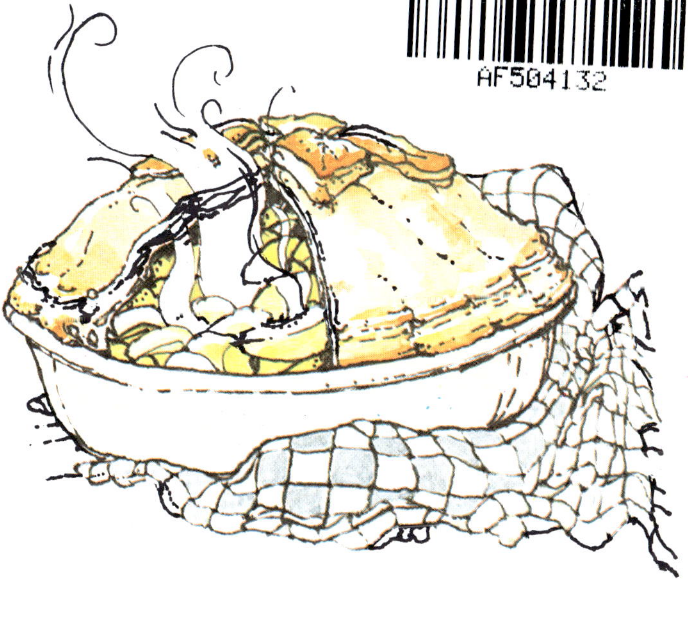

Sunday

Thank you for the world so sweet,
Thank you for the food we eat.
Thank you for the birds that sing,
Thank you, God, for everything.

Monday

All good gifts around us
Are sent from heaven above.
Then thank the Lord,
O thank the Lord
For all his love.

Thank you, Jesus,
for this food.
Amen.

Tuesday

God is great, God is good,
Thank you, God, for all our food.

Wednesday

For every cup and plateful,
God make us truly grateful.

For health and strength
and daily food
we praise your name
O Lord.

Thursday

For food and drink and happy days,
Accept our gratitude and praise;
In serving others, Lord, we do
Express our thankfulness to you.

Friday

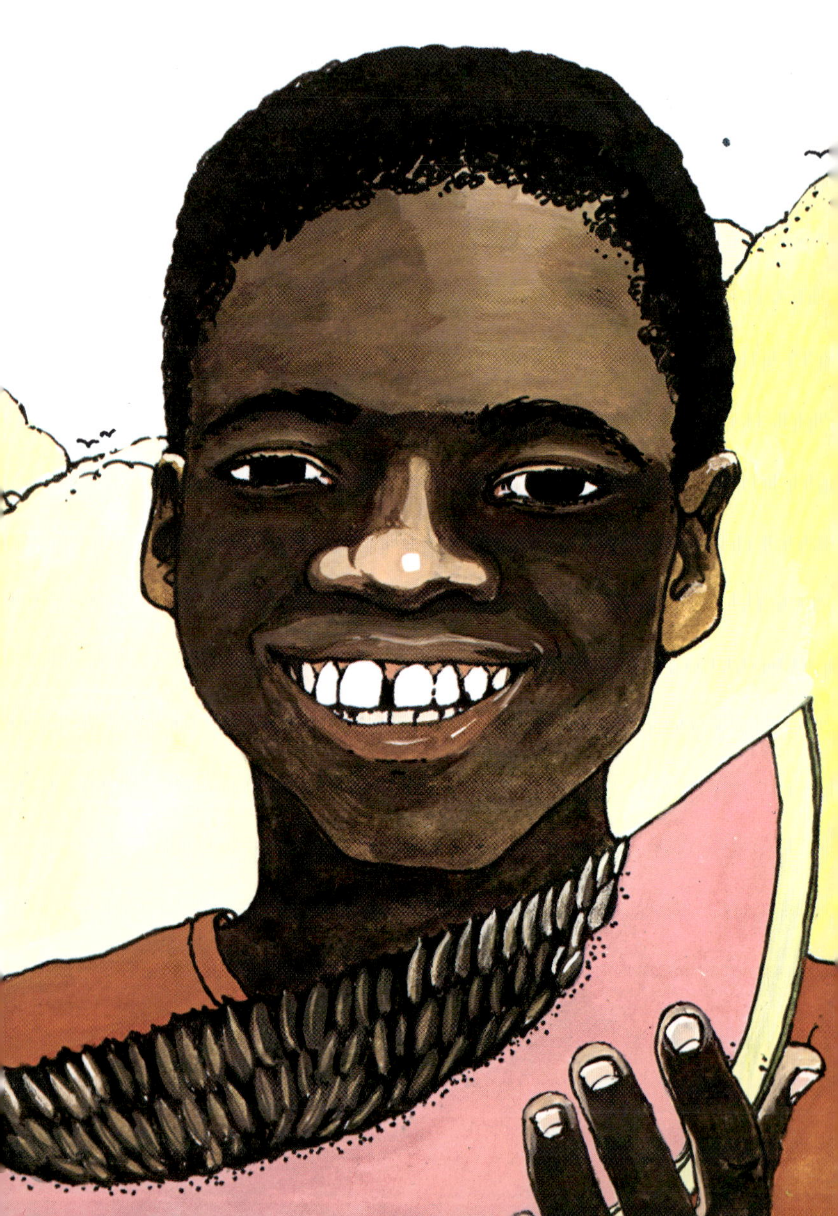

We thank you,
Father, for your care
For all your children everywhere.
As you feed us all our days
May our lives be filled with praise.

Saturday

Praise God
from whom all blessings flow,
Praise him,
all creatures here below,
Praise him above,
you heavenly host,
Praise Father,
Son and Holy Ghost.

Published by
Lion Publishing plc
Icknield Way, Tring, Herts, England
ISBN 0 85648 030 4
Lion Publishing Corporation
10885 Textile Road, Belleville, Michigan 48111, USA
ISBN 0 85648 030 4
Albatross Books
PO Box 320, Sutherland, NSW 2232, Australia
ISBN 0 86760 301 1

First edition 1975
Reprinted 1976, 1978, 1979, 1981, 1983, 1984, 1985

Printed and bound in Italy by
International Publishing Enterprises, Rome

Acknowledgments

'Thank you for the world so sweet' by E. Rutter Leatham from *Hymns and
Songs for Children*, The National Society. 'God is great, God is good' and
'For food and drink and happy days' from *Little Folded Hands*, Concordia
Publishing House Ltd. 'For every cup and plateful' from *An Anthology of
Prayers* by A. S. T. Fisher, Longman Group Ltd. 'For health and strength',
J. Curwen and Sons. 'We thank you, Father, for your care' by Rosalie
Wakefield from *A Brownie Guide Prayer Book*, SPCK.